MW01277324

JAMESTOWN

Heritage

READERS

Book B

Lee Mountain, Ed.D.
University of Houston, Texas

Sharon Crawley, Ed.D.
Florida Atlantic University

Edward Fry, Ph.D.
Professor Emeritus
Rutgers University

Jamestown Publishers
Providence, Rhode Island

Favorite Children's Classics

ILLUSTRATED BY THE BEST ARTISTS
FROM THE PAST AND PRESENT

Jamestown Heritage Readers, Book B
Catalog No. 952
Catalog No. 952H, Hardcover Edition

Cover and text design by Deborah Hulsey Christie
Cover and border illustrations by Pamela R. Levy

Printed in the United States of America

3   4   5   6   7   HA   97   96   95   94   93

ISBN 0-89061-952-2
ISBN 0-89061-711-2, Hardcover Edition

C·O·N·T·E·N·T·S

ONE
Tales Retold

T W O

Here and There, Then and Now

UNIT ONE
Tales Retold

How the Dog Got His Place by the Fire

from an African legend
retold by
KATHLEEN ARNOTT

Long ago the dog and the jackal lived together in the bush.

Each day they hunted.

Each night they ate together.

But one cold night both of them came back with no food.

"I am very hungry," said the dog. "And I am cold too."

"Go to sleep now," said the jackal. "We will hunt again in the morning. Maybe we will catch a deer."

The dog could not sleep.

He shook when the cold wind blew.
As the night grew darker, he saw a light
far away.

"Jackal," he said. "What is that light?"

The jackal looked. "That is a fire,"
he said, "a fire made by people."

"You are braver than I," said the dog.
"Won't you go and fetch me some fire?"

"No," said the jackal.

The dog was afraid of people.

But he kept thinking about the fire.
Maybe people were cooking food there.
Maybe they might leave bones nearby.

Maybe he could chew on the bones and warm himself by the fire.

The dog stood up. "Jackal," he said. "I am going to try to get near the fire. If I don't come back soon, call to me. That will help me find my way back to you."

Off ran the dog. Soon he was near the fire. He stepped closer and closer.

Just as he reached the fire, a man ran out of his hut.

The man caught him by the neck and said, "Why are you here?"

"Please don't hurt me," said the dog. "I am cold and hungry."

The dog was shaking.

"Please let me lie by your fire,"
he said.

The man felt sorry for him.

"You may lie by my fire," he said.
"But when you are warm, you must go
back to the bush."

Now the dog was happy.

Near him lay a bone that the man had thrown down.

He chewed on the bone, and the fire warmed him. Never had he felt so good!

The man called from his little hut, "Aren't you warm yet?"

"Not quite," said the dog.

He had just spotted another bone.

Soon the man asked again, "Dog, aren't you warm by now?"

But the dog thought of the cold wind out in the bush. "Let me stay just a bit longer," he said.

It was some time before the man called out again.

"You must be warm by now," he said.

The dog said, "Yes, I am warm now, but I do not want to go back to the bush. I am cold and hungry there."

17

The dog asked, "May I stay with you?"
The man did not answer right away.
"I will never kill your chickens,
the way the jackal does," the dog added.
"I will help you when you go hunting.
All I will ask is a bone to chew on and
a place by your fire."

The man knew that he could believe
what the dog was saying.

"Very well," he said. "You may stay.
If you will help me hunt, I will give you
food and a place by my fire."

Since that day, the dog has had
his place by the fire. Since that day,
people have given bones to dogs.

But sometimes at night you can hear the jackal calling.

He still calls from the bush, trying to get the dog to return to him.

But the dog never answers the call.

And the jackal stays in the bush and hunts alone.

When You Are As Hungry As the Dog

by

JACK LONDON

Throwing a leftover bone to the dog is not charity. Charity is sharing the bone with the dog when you are just as hungry as the dog.

Jack Sprat

from
MOTHER GOOSE

Jack Sprat could eat no fat.
His wife could eat no lean.
And so, between them both,
They licked the platter clean.

21

Thumbelina

by

HANS CHRISTIAN ANDERSEN

There was once a woman who made a wish. "I wish I had a tiny little girl," she said.

But she did not know where to find a tiny little girl.

So she asked a witch for help.

The witch gave her a seed to plant.

The little seed grew into a tall plant with a flower.

One day the flower opened.

There inside was a tiny little girl!

The little girl was not even as tall as your thumb.

The woman smiled.

"Here is the little girl I wished for," she said. "I will call her Thumbelina."

The woman gave her a pretty nutshell for a bed.

Each day Thumbelina saw the birds from her window.

She smiled to hear them sing.

She too could sing—more sweetly than a bird. She was very happy.

One night, when she was sleeping, Mrs. Toad hopped in the window.

She saw Thumbelina in her bed.

"What a pretty girl!" said Mrs. Toad. "My son can marry her."

Mrs. Toad picked up the tiny bed and hopped to the stream.

"See what I found for you," she said to her son.

Then they hopped away to get food.

Soon Thumbelina woke up.

She did not know where she was.

All day she tried to find her way home.

That night she came upon the door of a mouse house and knocked.

Old Mrs. Field Mouse let her in.

"Please help me," said Thumbelina. "I am lost."

"Oh, you poor thing," said Mrs. Field Mouse. "You can stay with me. I need someone who can cook and clean for me."

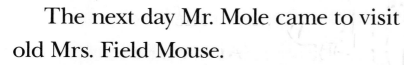

"Thank you!"
said Thumbelina.
"I will do all that you ask.
I will sing for you, too."

The next day Mr. Mole came to visit
old Mrs. Field Mouse.

She had Thumbelina sing for him.

He came back each day to hear her.
Mr. Mole made a tunnel from his home
to hers.

"I want you to use my tunnel," he told
Thumbelina. "You can walk through it
to come sing for me."

Thumbelina did not like the tunnel.
"It is too dark," she said.

Mr. Mole made a hole in the top
of the tunnel.

"Now you have some light," he said.

One day Thumbelina found a bird
lying in the tunnel.

He had fallen into the hole.

He was cold and still.

Thumbelina put her head against
his feathers. She could hear his heart.

She hurried to bring the bird a drop
of water on a leaf.

He opened his eyes.

"You have saved my life," he said.
"I hurt my wing and fell into here.
But soon I will be able to fly out."

"First you must get strong again," she said. "I will take care of you."

Thumbelina looked after the bird until he was well.

"Now come away with me," said the bird. "I will take you to a land where it is warm. You can play in the sun there."

Thumbelina sighed. How good it would be to feel the sun once more!

But she had told Mrs. Mouse that she would stay to cook and clean for her.

"You must go without me," she said to the bird.

"I will never forget you," the bird said. He flew out through the hole.

Thumbelina went back to the mouse house.

For a year she stayed and helped Mrs. Mouse.

Each time Mr. Mole came to visit, she would sing for him.

When fall came again, Mr. Mole said to Mrs. Field Mouse, "I wish to marry Thumbelina."

"Thumbelina," said Mrs. Field Mouse. "You must sew your wedding dress."

Thumbelina had to cut and sew, day and night.

The mole hired four spiders to spin for her, but she was not happy.

Thumbelina kept telling Mrs. Mouse she did not want to marry Mr. Mole.

"Stop saying that," said Mrs. Mouse. "He is a very fine mole. If you keep on crying about marrying him, I will bite you with my white teeth."

That frightened Thumbelina.

And because she was frightened,
she stayed outside of the mouse house
as much as she could.

The next day, when she was outside,
she heard a bird singing.

She looked up and waved.

It was Thumbelina's old friend,
the bird from the tunnel.

He said, "I am flying south again.
Won't you come with me this year?
I'll carry you on my back to the land
of the Flower Elves."

"Oh, yes!" said Thumbelina. "I will
go with you now."

She tied
herself to one
of his feathers.

Then up in the air
he flew. When they
came to the warm lands,
the sun was bright.

Thumbelina sang for joy as
the bird landed in a field of flowers.

"You can find a home for yourself
in one of these flowers," said the bird.
He put Thumbelina down on a leaf.

There on the leaf next to her stood
a little elf. He had a crown on his head.
And he was no bigger than Thumbelina.

He smiled at her. Thumbelina thought he had the nicest smile she had ever seen.

"I am the King of the Flower Elves," he said. "My people heard you singing as the bird brought you to us. We want you to be our queen."

He took a gold crown and put it on her head. "Will you stay with us?"

Thumbelina said "Yes" with all her heart. So she and the King were married, and lived happily ever after.

Happy Thought

by

ROBERT LOUIS STEVENSON

The world is so full
   Of a number of things,
I'm sure we should all
   Be as happy as kings.

What Is Pink?

by

CHRISTINA ROSSETTI

What is pink? A rose is pink
By the fountain's brink.

What is blue? The sky is blue
Where the clouds float through.

What is green? The grass is green
With small flowers between.

What is orange? Why, an orange,
Just an orange!

The Lion and the Mouse
from
AESOP'S FABLES

There was once a lion who was strong and proud.

One day, when he was sleeping, a mouse ran across his nose.

The lion woke up with a roar, and he caught the little mouse in his paw.

"Oh, King Lion!" cried the mouse. "Please don't kill me. Please let me go. The day may come when I can do a good turn for you."

The lion laughed. He did not think the little mouse could ever help him.

But he let the mouse go.

The next day some hunters came
into the woods. They put out a trap
of ropes to catch the lion.

That night the strong and proud lion
stepped into the trap.

He let out a roar that was heard far
and wide.

The mouse heard it and ran to him.

"King Lion," said the mouse. "Now I can do a good turn for you."

At once the mouse got to work. She bit at the ropes with her teeth.

Soon she had made a little hole.

She worked on and on, making the hole larger.

At last the lion could get out.

And that is how the little mouse showed the lion that this old saying is true.

A friend in need is a friend indeed.

Puss in Boots
by
CHARLES PERRAULT

Once upon a time there was a very
clever cat. The cat's master was poor.
He had no fields, and no fine clothes.
But he did have this very clever cat.

"Master," said the cat. "I can help you make your fortune. Just give me a bag and a pair of boots."

The young man smiled. "Good cat," he said. "Here are the boots and a bag. Now you can have a fine new name— Puss in Boots. But I do not see how you can help me make my fortune."

The cat pulled on the high boots. "In time, you will see, Master," he said.

Puss in Boots put food in his bag.

He placed it on the ground, wide open, to catch a rabbit. Then Puss in Boots lay in wait, pretending to be asleep.

Soon he bagged a rabbit. He killed it and got it ready for cooking.

Proud of his catch, Puss in Boots took it to the castle.

He made a low bow to the king.

"Good day, my King," he said. "I have brought you a rabbit. It is a gift from my master."

"Who is your master?" asked the king.

That second, Puss in Boots made up a new name for his master. "The Duke of Carabas is my master," he said.

"Tell the Duke of Carabas that I thank him," said the king.

The next day Puss in Boots caught a duck. He then made a gift of the duck to the king.

A few days later, he caught a goose. And again he told the king that it was a gift from the Duke of Carabas.

One day Puss in Boots found out
that the king and the princess were
going for a ride by the river.

45

The cat hurried back to his master. "If you do as I say, your fortune is made," said Puss in Boots. "Go for a swim in the river. Leave the rest to me."

"Very well," said his master. "But I don't know what can be the use of it."

While he was swimming, the king passed by.

Then Puss in Boots cried, "Help! The Duke of Carabas is drowning."

The king heard the cry and saw the cat who had so often brought him gifts. At once he sent his men to help.

As they pulled the Duke of Carabas out of the water, the cat ran to the king.

He said, "My King, two men
stole my master's clothes."

At once the king sent for a fine suit.
"It is my gift to your master," he told
Puss in Boots.

The young man smiled at his cat
as he put on the fine clothes.

The king asked him to ride along
in the coach.

Puss in Boots ran ahead and found
some farm workers cutting corn.

"Good people," said Puss in Boots.
"You must say that this field belongs
to the Duke of Carabas, or you will be
cut up into small pieces."

Then the king rode up.

He had the coach stop at the field.

"Who owns this cornfield?" he asked.

"The Duke of Carabas," the workers said. The cat's words made them afraid.

They did not want to be cut up into small pieces.

The king rode on.

Again Puss in Boots ran ahead. He said the same thing to all he met.

The king was surprised at how much land the duke owned.

At last Puss in Boots came to a castle. It was the castle of a big, ugly Ogre.

The Ogre owned all the lands that the king had passed. Puss in Boots had taken care to learn all about this Ogre.

He bowed to the Ogre. "I hear that you can turn yourself into any animal you wish," he said. "Is that true?"

49

"It is true," said the Ogre.

He turned himself into a lion.

"Very good," said Puss in Boots. He tried not to sound as frightened as he felt. "But could you also turn yourself into something tiny? Could you become, say, a mouse?"

"Yes, I can do that," said the Ogre. And he turned himself into a mouse. But as he ran across the floor, Puss in Boots jumped on him and ate him up.

Just then the king reached the Ogre's castle.

Puss in Boots opened the door.

"Good day," said the cat. "Come into my master's castle."

The king went in first.

Then the Duke of Carabas gave his hand to the princess. He led her into the castle.

The king turned to the young man. "Your castle would be a fine home for my daughter," said the king. "And you would be a fine new son for me."

That same day the Duke of Carabas married the princess.

He gave his cat a new suit and a hat with a feather. And Puss in Boots never ran after mice any more.

Jack and the Bean Stalk

from an English folktale
by
JOSEPH JACOBS

Once there was a woman who was very poor. She had a son named Jack and a cow named Milky White.

One day she said, "Jack, we have no money for food. So you must sell Milky White."

On his way to town Jack met a man.

"Good day, my boy," said the man. "And where are you going?"

"I am going to town," said Jack. "I have to sell our cow."

"I'll give you five beans for the cow," said the man.

Jack laughed. "Why would I sell Milky White for five beans?"

"These are magic beans," the man said. "Plant them at night. By morning they will have grown up to the sky."

Jack gave the man the cow.

He took the beans and ran home.

"Mother," called Jack. "Look what I got for our cow. Magic beans!"

"You gave away Milky White for five beans!" cried his mother.

She threw the beans out the window. "No supper for you tonight."

How sad and sorry Jack was!

But early the next morning, he looked out his window and saw a giant bean stalk. So the beans were magic! Jack climbed to the top of the bean stalk.

There he saw a great big tall house. At the door was a woman.

"Good day," said Jack. "I'm hungry. Could you give me some breakfast?"

"It's breakfast you want, is it?" said the woman. "It's breakfast you'll be if you don't get away now."

"Why?" asked Jack.

"Because my man is a giant," she said. "He grinds up boys' bones."

"Why would he do that?" asked Jack.

"Oh, he just loves bread baked with ground bones in it," said the woman. "He always tries to catch English boys from the land under us."

"Well," said Jack. "I may as well be ground up as stay this hungry."

The giant's wife gave him some cakes. While he was eating, he heard a noise.

Thump! THUMP! THUMP!

"That's my man!" said the giant's wife. "Quick! Jump into the oven."

The house shook as the giant came in.

"Cook my breakfast, Wife," he roared. Then he sniffed. "What's this I smell?

Fe, fi, fo, fum!
I smell the blood of an English man.
Be he alive or be he dead,
I'll grind his bones to make my bread."

"How you do go on," said his wife.
"Do you see an English man here?
Do you even see an English boy?
I'll get breakfast ready for you."

After breakfast the giant took out
a bag of gold. He counted his money
until he went to sleep.

Then Jack jumped out of the oven.
He grabbed the bag of gold and ran out
the door.

Jack climbed down the bean stalk.

He was home with the gold before
the giant woke up.

Jack and his mother lived on the gold for some time. When the gold was gone, he climbed the stalk again.

Again he went to the big tall house. Again he saw the giant's wife.

"Aren't you the boy who came here before?" she asked. "You know, that day my man missed one of his bags of gold."

Before Jack could answer her, they heard the giant coming.

Thump! THUMP! THUMP!

Jack hid behind the door.

The giant came in and wanted his breakfast. Then he sniffed.

"Fe, fi, fo, fum!
  I smell the blood of an English man.
  Be he alive or be he dead,
  I'll grind his bones to make my bread."

But his wife just shook her head and gave him breakfast.

Then he said, "Wife, bring me the hen that lays the golden eggs."

Jack peeked out from behind the door.

Soon the giant took a nap.

Jack tiptoed over and picked up the hen. Then he was off and down the bean stalk.

His mother was very happy with a golden egg each day.

But Jack wanted to try his luck again.
So one day he climbed the bean stalk
still another time. This time he hid
behind a chair in the giant's house.

The giant came in for breakfast. He
sniffed. "I smell something," he cried.

"Fe, fi, fo, fum!
I smell the blood of an English man.
Be he alive or be he dead,
I'll grind his bones to make my bread."

The giant's wife looked in her oven.
But Jack was not there. So she said, "I
don't know what you smell. Sit down
and eat your breakfast."

After he ate, the giant got his golden harp. He said, "Play for me, Harp."

The golden harp played until the giant fell asleep.

Jack stepped out from behind the chair. He picked up the harp.

But just as Jack got to the door, the harp called out,

"Help! HELP!"

The giant woke up and saw Jack running away with the harp.

He jumped up and ran after Jack.

Jack leaped onto the bean stalk and started down.

63

The giant stopped for a second. The bean stalk looked too light to hold him. Then the harp called again,

"Help! HELP!"

And the giant started down after Jack.

When Jack was near the ground, he called, "Mother, bring me an ax."

And she did—just as the giant's feet were coming through the clouds.

Jack grabbed the ax. Chop! Chop! The bean stalk tumbled over.

So the giant fell down and broke his crown. And the bean stalk came tumbling after.

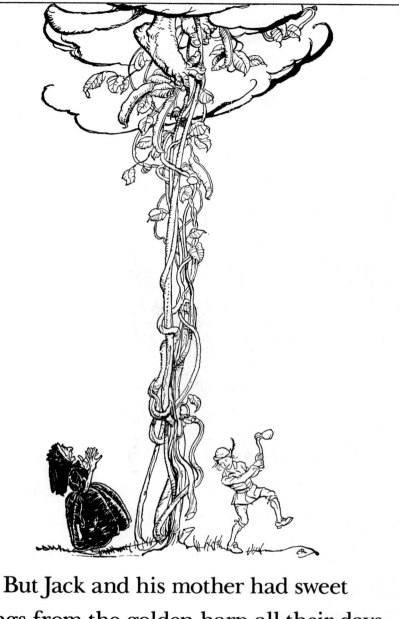

But Jack and his mother had sweet
songs from the golden harp all their days.

The Frog Prince

by the

BROTHERS GRIMM

Once upon a time there lived a king.
He had a fair, young daughter.

The king had given her a golden ball.
She played with it every day.

The king and his daughter lived near
a dark forest. And there, under a tree,
was a deep well.

When the day was warm, the princess
would sit by the well.

There she would play with her ball.

One day, as the princess threw her golden ball in the air, it did not fall into her hands. It fell into the well. Splash!

The well was deep. The princess was sure she would never see her ball again. So she cried and cried and could not stop.

"What is the matter?" said a voice behind her.

The girl looked around, and she saw a frog. He was in the well, sticking his head out of the water.

"Oh, it's you—you old water splasher," said the girl. "My ball fell into the well."

"I can help," said the frog. "I can get your ball. What will you give me if I do?"

"Whatever you wish," said the girl. "I'll give you my fine golden ring. I'll bring you flowers from my garden."

"I do not want your fine golden ring or flowers from your garden," said the frog. "But I would like to live with you and be your friend."

He went on, "I would like to eat from your dish and drink from your cup. I would like to sleep on your bed. If I get your ball, will you promise me all this, Princess?"

"Oh, yes," said the princess. "I'll promise." But she thought, "Silly frog! He could never live with me."

When the frog heard her promise, he went down in the well.

He soon came up with the golden ball in his mouth. He dropped it on the grass at her feet.

She laughed when she saw the ball. Then she picked it up and ran off.

"Wait," cried the frog. "Wait for me. Take me with you."

But she did not listen. She just ran home. She soon forgot the poor frog.

That night the princess was eating dinner when—plop-plop, plop-plop—something came climbing up the steps.

When it reached the door, it knocked. It cried out in a loud voice.

"Daughter of the King,
Open the door for me."

The princess ran to the door. There was the frog, wet and green and cold! She slammed the door in his face.

The king saw that she was afraid.

He said, "My daughter, what are you afraid of?"

"It's a fat, old frog," said the princess.

"And what does he want of you?" asked the king.

"Oh, Father, my ball fell into the well. The frog brought it back to me. So I promised him he could be my friend.

But I never thought he would leave his well. I said he could eat from my dish and drink from my cup. I even said he could sleep in my bed."

The girl shuddered. "But I couldn't stand that, Papa. He's so wet and cold." The frog knocked again and said,

"Daughter of the King,
Open the door for me.
You promised I could
be your friend.
Open the door for me."

At that, the king said, "You know that if you make promises, you must keep them. So you had better open the door."

The princess knew that she had to do as her father said. She opened the door.

The frog said, "Pick me up. I wish to sit by you at the table."

She shook her head and turned away.

But her father looked at her and said, "You must keep your promise."

Then the frog said, "Now push your dish close to me."

Again the princess looked away. But she had to do it. The frog ate and ate, but the girl could not eat a thing.

At last the frog said, "I feel tired. Take me to your room. I want to go to sleep now."

The princess looked at her father. It had been bad enough to have to touch the frog. But to have him on her bed was more than she could bear.

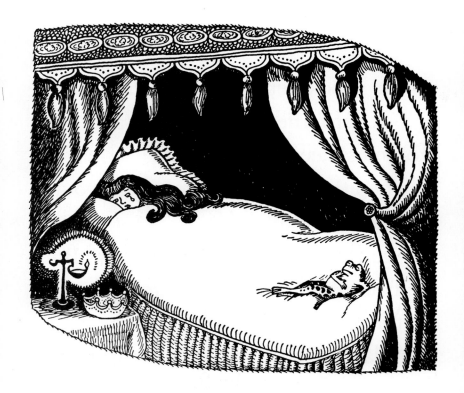

The king said, "The frog helped you in your time of need. Is it fair to break your promise to him now?"

The princess was angry. But she put the frog at the foot of her bed.

Then she cried herself to sleep.

When morning came, the frog jumped down and went away. She did not know where.

The next night it was the same. The frog came back. He knocked at the door, and she had to let him in.

Again he ate out of her dish, and he drank from her golden cup. Again he went to sleep at the foot of her bed.

In the morning he went away as he had before.

The third night he said, "I want to sleep at the head of your bed. I think I would like it better there."

The girl thought she would never be able to sleep with a cold, wet frog near her face.

But she put him there. Then she cried herself to sleep again.

In the morning the frog hopped off the bed. But as soon as his feet touched the floor, something happened.

He was no longer a cold, green frog, but a young prince!

"I was not what I seemed to be!" he said to the princess. "I was turned into a frog by magic. No one but you could help me. Only if you kept your promise could I turn back into a prince."

He smiled. "I waited and waited at the well for you to help me."

The princess was so surprised she did not know what to say.

"Will you let me be your friend now?" said the prince, laughing. "You promised."

The princess laughed too.

For years they were the best of friends. And it is not hard to guess what happened when they grew up. They were married and lived happily ever after.

Happily Ever After?

by

ORLANDO BUSINO

"I WAS HAPPIER WHEN I WAS A FROG!"

The Frog

by

HILAIRE BELLOC

Be kind and tender to the frog,

79

And do not call him names,
As "Slimy-skin" or "Polly-wog,"
Or likewise, "Ugly James."

No animal will more repay
A treatment kind and fair.
At least, so lonely people say

Who keep a frog (and, by the way,
They are extremely rare).

UNIT TWO

Here and There, Then and Now

Nonsense A B C Rhymes
by
EDWARD LEAR

A was an ape,
Who stole some white tape,
And tied up his toes
In four beautiful bows.

B was a bat,
Who slept all day,
And fluttered about
When the sun went away.

C was a camel.
You rode on his hump.
And if you fell off,
You came down with a bump.

How the Camel Got His Hump

by

RUDYARD KIPLING

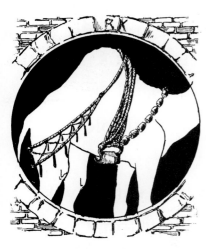

When the world was new and the animals were just beginning to work, there was a camel. When anyone asked him to work, he said, "Humph!" Just "Humph!" and no more.

The horse came to him with a saddle on his back. He said, "Camel, oh, Camel! Come out and trot like the rest of us."

"Humph!" said the camel.

And the horse went away and told the man.

Then the dog came to him with a stick. He said, "Camel, oh, Camel! Come and fetch like the rest of us."

"Humph!" said the camel.

And the dog went away and told the man.

Soon the ox came to him with a yoke on his neck. He said, "Camel, oh, Camel! Come and plow like the rest of us."

"Humph!" said the camel. And the ox went away and told the man.

At the end of three days the man called the horse, the dog, and the ox.

He said, "My animals, I am sorry, but that humph-thing in the desert won't work. So you must work harder to make up for him."

The animals were angry. They met to talk about what should be done.

The camel came by and laughed. He said, "Humph," and walked away.

Soon the Wizard of the Desert came to talk with the animals.

"Wizard, is it right for someone to be idle?" asked the horse.

"No," said the Wizard.

"Well," said the horse. "There is
a thing in your desert with a long neck.
He hasn't done a bit of work in the three
days that we have been working. And
he won't trot."

"Whew!" said the Wizard. "That is
bad. But that's the camel. What does he
say about it?"

"He says, 'Humph!' " said the dog.
"And he won't fetch."

"Does he say anything else?" asked
the Wizard.

"Only 'Humph!' " said the ox. "And
he won't plow."

"Very well," said the Wizard.

"I'll humph him," the Wizard added.
Soon he found the camel.

"Humph!" said the camel.

"My long-legged friend," said the
Wizard. "Why don't you work?"

"Humph!" said the camel.

The Wizard sat
down with his
head in his
hands.

He began to think a great magic.

"You've given the horse, the dog, and the ox more work because you are idle," said the Wizard.

"Humph!" said the camel.

"I would not say that again if I were you," said the Wizard. "You might say it once too often. I want you to work."

The camel said, "Humph!" again. But no sooner had he said it than he saw his back puffing up and puffing up.

It puffed all the way up into a great big humph. (We call it a "hump" now.)

"That's your very own hump," said the Wizard. "Now you will work."

"How can I
with this hump
on my back?"
said the camel.

"That hump will help you work," said the Wizard.

"You missed three days of work with the horse, the dog, and the ox. But now you can work for three days without eating, because you can live on your hump. So, go to work now. And behave!"

So the camel went, hump and all, to work with the horse, the dog, and the ox.

From that day to this, the camel
wears a hump. He has never caught up
on the three days of work he missed
at the beginning of the world. And
he has never yet learned to behave.

The camel's hump is an ugly lump
Which well you may see at the zoo.
But uglier yet is the hump we get
From having too little to do.

I get it as well as you-oo-oo.
If I haven't enough to do-oo-oo.
    We all get the hump,
    The idleness hump,
Kiddies and grown-ups too!

Facts about Camels

from encyclopedias

Can a camel really work for days with nothing to eat? Can it use its hump for food? Does it need much water? Does it really hate to work?

To answer those questions, look up the word "camel" in an encyclopedia. That book will give you facts about camels.

Rudyard Kipling used some facts in his story "How the Camel Got His Hump." At the end of his story, the Wizard tells the camel, "You can live on your hump." The camel really can live on the food in its hump.

The hump is mostly a pile of fat that the camel uses for food. Camels can go for weeks with no food or water. So the camel can live on the food in its hump. That's a fact.

The Wizard also told the camel to behave. People still try to get the camel to behave.

Camels still don't seem to like people. They don't seem to like animals either. At the zoo you may see a camel bite another animal.

A camel makes noises when you pile things on its back. It puffs heavily as it gets to its feet. It will carry things if it must. But it still does not like to work.

As Rudyard Kipling said in his story, the camel has never learned to behave.

At the Zoo

by

WILLIAM MAKEPEACE THACKERAY

First I saw the white bear.
 Then I saw the black.
Then I saw the camel
 with a hump upon its back.
Then I saw the elephant
 a-waving of its trunk.
Then I saw the monkeys—how
 unpleasantly they—smelled!

97

The Pledge to the Flag

by

LEE MOUNTAIN

Class

> What do you mean
> By the words you say
> When you talk to the flag
> Of the USA?

Uncle Sam

> Talk to the flag?
> That is not what I do.
> I pledge allegiance
> And so can you.

Class

> "Pledge" is a word
> We never have seen.
> And, tell us, what
> Does "allegiance" mean?

Uncle Sam

To pledge means to promise
Just what you will do.
When you promise allegiance
You pledge to be true.

BETSY ROSS MAKING THE FLAG
(THE FIRST STARS AND STRIPES)

Girls

> When pledging allegiance
> We always stand,
> To show that we love
> And respect our land.

Boys

> Uncle Sam,
> We think we've guessed
> Why you say the Pledge
> With your hand on your chest.
> You take this position
> Before you start
> To show that the words
> Come right from your heart.

Uncle Sam

> I will teach you more.
> Cover hearts with hands.
> "And to the republic
> For which it stands.
> One nation, indivisible—"

Girls

Wait, Uncle Sam!
What in creation
Is meant by
An "indivisible" nation?

JOHN PAUL JONES HOISTS OUR FIRST FLAG
(THE GRAND UNION FLAG)

Uncle Sam

We're a grouping of states
That right from the start
Could not be divided
Or broken apart.

Boys

The rest of the Pledge
Is saying to you
That you will have justice
And liberty too.

Uncle Sam

Justice for all
Means fairness, you see,
And liberty means
You will always be free.

Class

We understand the Pledge
All the way through.
So now we will say it
By heart for you.

The Pledge of Allegiance

I pledge allegiance to the flag
of the United States of America
and to the republic for which it stands,
one nation, under God, indivisible,
with liberty and justice for all.

OLD GLORY, SYMBOL OF LIBERTY

(THE STARS AND STRIPES)

Chicken Little

A PLAY

adapted from an English folktale

Characters

Narrator

Chicken Little

Henny Penny

Ducky Lucky

Goosey Loosey

Turkey Lurkey

Foxy Woxy

Narrator   Once upon a time Chicken Little walked by a chestnut tree. And just as she did, a chestnut fell on her tail. She was frightened. So she ran to Henny Penny.

Chicken Little   Oh, Henny Penny! The sky is falling.

Henny Penny   How do you know?

Chicken Little   I saw it with my eyes. I heard it with my ears. And part of it fell on my tail.

Henny Penny   Let's run and tell the King.

Narrator   On the way they met Ducky Lucky.

Chicken Little   Oh, Ducky Lucky! The sky is falling.

Ducky Lucky   How do you know?

Chicken Little   I saw it with my eyes. I heard it with my ears. And part of it fell on my tail.

Ducky Lucky   Let's run and tell the King.

Narrator   On the way they met Goosey Loosey.

Chicken Little   Oh, Goosey Loosey! The sky is falling.

Goosey Loosey   How do you know?

Chicken Little   I saw it with my eyes. I heard it with my ears. And part of it fell on my tail.

Goosey Loosey   Let's run and tell the King.

Narrator   On the way they met Turkey Lurkey.

106

Chicken Little Oh, Turkey Lurkey! The sky is falling.

Turkey Lurkey How do you know?

Chicken Little I saw it with my eyes. I heard it with my ears. And part of it fell on my tail.

Turkey Lurkey Let's run and tell the King.

Narrator On the way they met Foxy Woxy.

Chicken Little Oh, Foxy Woxy! The sky is falling.

Foxy Woxy How do you know?

Chicken Little I saw it with my eyes. I heard it with my ears. And part of it fell on my tail. We are running to tell the King.

Foxy Woxy Oh, so that is where you are going! Well, the King lives on the other side of the hill. And I know where a tunnel goes through the hill. Come with me. I'll show you.

Narrator They followed Foxy Woxy, who was up to no good. He took them to the mouth of the tunnel.

Foxy Woxy This is where the tunnel starts. But it is not very wide. Let me take you through, one at a time. You come with me first, Henny Penny.

Henny Penny Very well. But it does look dark in there.

Narrator   They went into the tunnel. Ducky Lucky, Goosey Loosey, Turkey Lurkey, and Chicken Little waited for Foxy Woxy to come back. Soon he returned, looking very pleased with himself.

Foxy Woxy   Now I will take you, Ducky Lucky. Come along.

Ducky Lucky   Very well. But I am afraid of the dark.

Foxy Woxy   Are you now? Well, don't be afraid. I'll take care of you. Good care! Heh, heh, heh!

109

Narrator   They went into the tunnel. Goosey Loosey, Turkey Lurkey, and Chicken Little waited for Foxy Woxy to come back. Soon he returned, looking very pleased again.

Foxy Woxy   Now I will take you, Goosey Loosey.

Goosey Loosey   Very well. But let's get through the tunnel quickly.

Foxy Woxy   We will. We will. Just come with me.

Narrator   They went into the tunnel. Turkey Lurkey and Chicken Little waited for Foxy Woxy to come back. Soon he returned, looking as pleased as could be.

Foxy Woxy   Now it is your turn, Turkey Lurkey.

Turkey Lurkey   But maybe I'm too big around to get through the tunnel.

Foxy Woxy   No indeed. You will fit. Heh, heh!

Narrator   They went into the tunnel. Chicken Little waited for Foxy Woxy to come back. All at once, a chestnut fell to the ground, right beside her.

Chicken Little   Oh, dear! The sky is falling again. But wait! No, it's not! The sky is not falling. It's chestnuts that are falling. Oh, I must catch up with my friends and tell them.

Narrator   Chicken Little ran into the tunnel, just in time to see Foxy Woxy pushing Turkey Lurkey into a bag. She ran out again and flew up into the chestnut tree.

111

Chicken Little I must help my
   friends. Just wait until Foxy Woxy
   comes out again! I'll fix him. I'm
   going to scare him away.

Narrator Chicken Little gathered lots
   of chestnuts and watched for Foxy
   Woxy. Soon he returned and looked
   around for her. But he could not
   see her up in the tree. She dropped
   all her chestnuts on him.

Foxy Woxy Help! Help! The sky
   really is falling!

Narrator   Foxy Woxy ran away. Chicken Little went into the tunnel and let her friends out of the fox's bag. All four birds went back to the chestnut tree.

Chicken Little   We don't need to run and tell the King that the sky is falling. It was just a chestnut that fell on my tail. But we could run and tell the King how I got the best of Foxy Woxy.

Narrator   And that is just what they did.

Time to Rise

by

ROBERT LOUIS STEVENSON

A birdie with a yellow bill
Hopped upon the window sill,
Cocked his shining eye and said,
"Ain't you 'shamed, you sleepy-head!"

Hugh Idle

by

NATHANIEL HAWTHORNE

Hugh Idle did not like work of any kind. He was so lazy that his mother and father did not know what to do about him. At last they sent him away to school, hoping he would learn to work.

His school was run by a teacher named Mr. Toil. Mr. Toil was cross with lazy boys, so Hugh did not like him. Mr. Toil made Hugh work in class.

One day Hugh thought, "I don't like it here. I think I'll run away from school."

The next morning he ran down the road as fast as he could. But as soon as he was out of sight of the school, Hugh slowed down.

He smiled. Now he had nothing to do, so he could take his time.

He saw a man ahead of him. The man turned and said, "Good morning, my boy. Where might you be going?"

"I have run away from school," he said. "My teacher, Mr. Toil, made me work hard, and I did not like that."

"I see," said the man. "Well, you can come along with me. I know Mr. Toil, so I know how hard he would want you to work."

They walked on and came to a field where some farmers were at work.

Hugh stopped by a stone wall.

"How nice it must be to cut hay in the sun!" he said.

"Ah, but cutting hay is hard work," said the man.

"Oh," said Hugh. "Then I would not like it."

All at once Hugh started back from the wall. "Quick! Quick!" he cried. "Let us run, or he will catch me."

"Who?" asked the man, surprised.

"Mr. Toil!" answered Hugh. "Don't you see him?"

Hugh pointed at the farmer who
was telling the others what to do.

He looked just like Mr. Toil.

"That is not Mr. Toil," the man said.
"That is a brother of his who is a farmer.
He won't trouble you, unless you go to
work on his farm."

119

They walked on and came to a spot where some men were building a house.

"Let's stop here," said Hugh. "Let's watch these men work."

All of a sudden Hugh was frightened. "There is Mr. Toil again," he cried.

Hugh pointed at a man who was marking out the work.

"Oh, no," said his friend. "That is not Mr. Toil. That is a friend of his who builds homes."

"I am very glad to hear it," said Hugh. "But if you please, sir, I should still like to get out of his way."

So Hugh Idle and his friend hurried away. Soon Hugh slowed down. He was too tired to keep running. He stopped again when they saw some soldiers.

"If only I could be a soldier," thought Hugh. "I could go off and be in parades, and Mr. Toil would never catch me."

121

"Quick step!" shouted a loud voice.

Hugh jumped. The voice sounded just like the one he heard each day in Mr. Toil's class. And the soldier who shouted looked just like Mr. Toil.

"Come! We must get away," he cried. "Mr. Toil will put me to work."

Hugh's friend shook his head. "That soldier is not your teacher," he said.

"But he sounds just like Mr. Toil," said Hugh. "I want to get away."

"Very well," said his friend, and he led the way down the road.

Hugh had to trot to keep up with the man. He longed to stop and rest.

On and on they went, until Hugh was too tired to take one more step. He sat down on the road.

"Take me back," he cried. "All day I have seen Mr. Toil everywhere I looked. Running away is harder than working. I wish I were back at my school."

123

"There is your school," said the man.

He and Hugh had been walking for hours, but they had gone in a circle. "Come. I will go back with you."

Something about the man's voice made Hugh look up. And when he looked into his friend's eyes—behold!

There was Mr. Toil! And this man was truly Mr. Toil, his teacher.

But this time Hugh did not run away.

"I'm ready," he said. "I'm ready to do my work."

A Diller, A Dollar

from
MOTHER GOOSE

A diller, a dollar,

A ten o'clock scholar!

What makes you come so soon?

You used to come at ten o'clock.

But now you come at noon.

125

10

The Fox and the Stork

from
AESOP'S FABLES

The fox loved to play tricks.

He once invited the stork to dinner. "Come over at six," said the fox.

The hungry stork was right on time. She could hardly wait to eat.

The fox brought out a shallow dish of soup and set it between them.

"What fine soup!" said the fox as he lapped up every drop.

But the stork could only wet the end of her long bill in the shallow dish.

So she left as hungry as she came.

The next week the stork invited the fox to dinner. "Come over at six," she said.

The hungry fox was right on time.

The stork set out a tall jar of soup.

She stuck her long sharp bill in the jar.

"What fine soup!" she said.

But the fox could not fit his mouth in the jar. So he left as hungry as he came.

If you play tricks on others, they will play tricks on you.

Animal Crackers

by

CHRISTOPHER MORLEY

Animal crackers and cocoa to drink,
That is the finest of suppers, I think.
When I'm grown up
   and can have what I please
I think I shall always insist upon these.

In the Cave of the One-Eyed Giant

from the
ODYSSEY
by
HOMER

My true name is Odysseus. But I once used another name. That name saved my life. I will tell you the story.

I was sailing home from Troy with my men. Strong winds blew our ship into strange waters. We reached land, but it was a land we did not know.

So I took ten men with me to go exploring. We came upon a huge cave.

We found no one inside, but there were huge cheeses and pails of milk.

"We will wait and find out what kind of man lives here," I said. "Maybe we can be friends with this man."

But that was not to be. For as soon as my men saw him coming, they ran. They tried to hide from him in the back of the cave.

He was a giant, three times taller than I am. He had one eye. That eye was in the middle of his forehead.

I had heard tales of one-eyed giants called Cyclopes. They were fierce and wild. I feared for my men.

This Cyclops drove ten huge sheep into the cave and milked them.

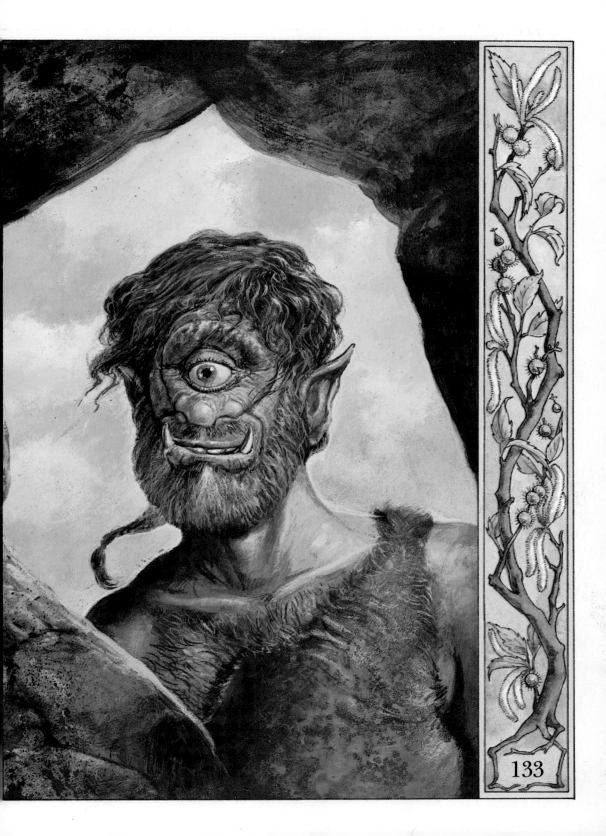

Then he took up a heavy rock and set it in the mouth of the cave. It closed out the daylight, so the one-eyed giant lit his fire. And by the light of that fire, he saw us.

I spoke to him and asked for food for my men.

He answered me by picking up two of my men and banging their heads on the ground.

Then he ate them!

"Tell me your name, oh leader of these men," said the Cyclops. "Tell me your name so that I may thank you for this fine lunch that I have eaten. What is your name?"

135

A plan started to form in my mind.

I answered him slowly. "My name
is Noman," I said.

My men looked at me strangely. They
knew that my true name was Odysseus.
But they said nothing.

"Then I will call you Noman," said the
Cyclops. "And I will eat two more of your
men after my nap, Noman," he added.
Then he lay down and went to sleep.

My first wish was to take my sword
and try to kill him right then.

But second thoughts held me back.
Even if I could do this, how would we
get out of the cave?

137

My men and I could not roll away
the huge stone at the door.

But a plan was growing in my mind.

I waited until he was in a deep sleep.
Then I grabbed my sword, rushed at
him, and thrust it in his eye.

He raised a cry that made the rocks
ring. His cries brought other Cyclopes
to the mouth of the cave. They called out
and asked him what hurt him.

"Noman!" he yelled. "Noman hurt me."

One of them said, "If no man hurt you,
you should not have raised such a cry."

"Listen!" he shouted. "I tell you
Noman caused this pain in my eye."

138

"If no man caused it, it will soon go away," said the Cyclopes outside the cave.

"Noman will pay for this," shouted the giant, reaching around in the cave. "I wish to punish Noman. I wish to kill Noman. I wish to eat Noman."

The other Cyclopes walked away.

All this while, I had been hiding my men, one under each sheep. The wool was thick on the sheep's bellies.

Each man could hang on to that wool and not be found.

The Cyclops sat at the mouth of the cave to block the way. He rolled back the stone just enough for his sheep to get by.

139

He laid his hands on each one's back as it passed.

"My good sheep," he said. "Why do you walk so slowly? Is it because you are sad for your master? Ah, if you could talk, you would tell me where Noman is hiding. Then I would tear him apart and eat him."

The last sheep went by him. I was hanging on to the wool of its belly.

When that sheep had gone a little way from the cave, I let go of its wool and caught up with my men.

We ran back to our ship and set off.

When we were a good way out on the water, I shouted to the giant. "If anyone asks you again who set his mark on you, do not say it was Noman. That is not my name. Say it was Odysseus."

141

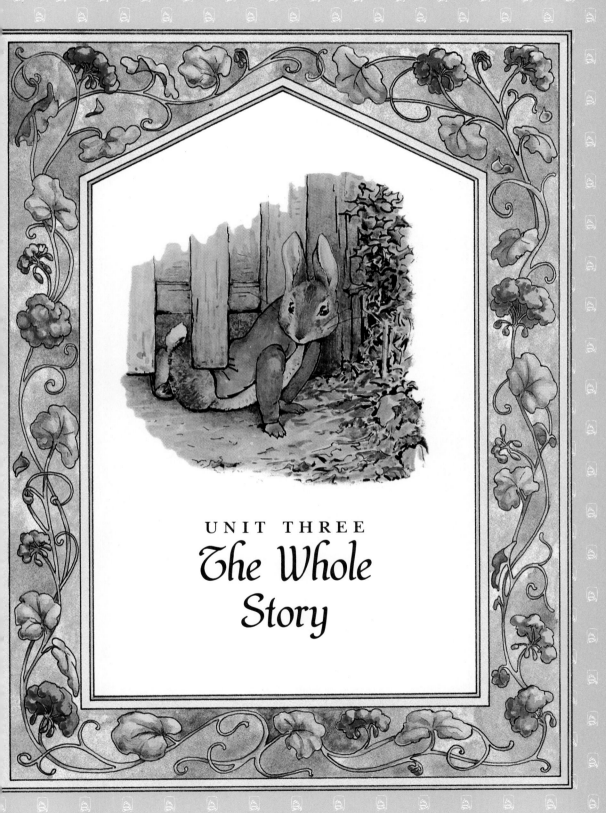

UNIT THREE

The Whole Story

The Tale of Peter Rabbit

story and pictures by
BEATRIX POTTER

Once upon a time there were four little Rabbits, and their names were—

Flopsy,

Mopsy,

Cotton-tail,

and Peter.

They lived with their Mother in a sand-bank, underneath the root of a very big fir-tree.

"Now, my dears," said old
Mrs. Rabbit one morning, "you may
go into the fields or down the lane,
but don't go into Mr. McGregor's garden:
your Father had an accident there;
he was put in a pie by Mrs. McGregor."

"Now run along, and don't get into
mischief. I am going out."

Then old Mrs. Rabbit took a basket
and her umbrella, and went through the
wood to the baker's. She bought a loaf
of brown bread and five currant buns.

Flopsy, Mopsy, and Cotton-tail,
who were good little bunnies, went
down the lane to gather blackberries.

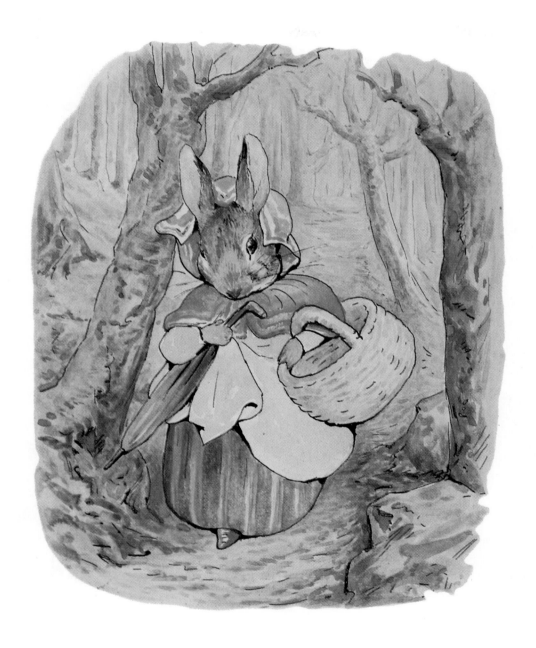

But Peter, who was very naughty, ran straight away to Mr. McGregor's garden, and squeezed under the gate!

First he ate some lettuces and some French beans; and then he ate some radishes;

And then, feeling rather sick, he went to look for some parsley.

But round the end of a cucumber frame, whom should he meet but Mr. McGregor!

Mr. McGregor was on his hands and knees planting out young cabbages, but he jumped up and ran after Peter, waving a rake and calling out, "Stop thief!"

Peter was most dreadfully frightened; he rushed all over the garden, for he had forgotten the way back to the gate.

He lost one of his shoes among the cabbages, and the other shoe amongst the potatoes.

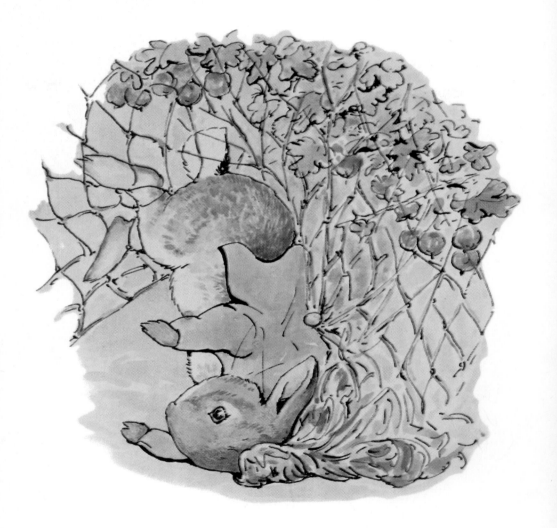

After losing them, he ran on four legs and went faster, so that I think he might have got away altogether if he had not unfortunately run into a gooseberry net, and got caught by the large buttons on his jacket. It was a blue jacket with brass buttons, quite new.

Peter gave himself up for lost, and shed big tears; but his sobs were overheard by some friendly sparrows, who flew to him in great excitement, and implored him to exert himself.

Mr. McGregor came up with a sieve, which he intended to pop upon the top of Peter; but Peter wriggled out just in time, leaving his jacket behind him.

And rushed into the tool-shed, and jumped into a can. It would have been a beautiful thing to hide in, if it had not had so much water in it.

Mr. McGregor was quite sure that Peter was somewhere in the tool-shed, perhaps hidden underneath a flower-pot. He began to turn them over carefully, looking under each.

Presently Peter sneezed—
"Kertyschoo!" Mr. McGregor was after
him in no time.

And tried to put his foot upon Peter,
who jumped out of a window, upsetting
three plants. The window was too small
for Mr. McGregor, and he was tired of
running after Peter. He went back to
his work.

Peter sat down to rest; he was out of
breath and trembling with fright, and
he had not the least idea which way to
go. Also he was very damp with sitting
in that can.

After a time he began to wander about, going lippity—lippity—not very fast, and looking all round.

He found a door in a wall; but it was locked, and there was no room for a fat little rabbit to squeeze underneath.

An old mouse was running in and out over the stone doorstep, carrying peas and beans to her family in the wood. Peter asked her the way to the gate, but she had such a large pea in her mouth that she could not answer. She only shook her head at him. Peter began to cry.

Then he tried to find his way straight across the garden, but he became more and more puzzled. Presently, he came to a pond where Mr. McGregor filled his water-cans. A white cat was staring at some gold-fish, she sat very, very still, but now and then the tip of her tail twitched as if it were alive. Peter thought it best to go away without speaking to her; he had heard about cats from his cousin, little Benjamin Bunny.

He went back towards the tool-shed, but suddenly, quite close to him, he heard the noise of a hoe—scr-r-ritch, scratch, scratch, scritch. Peter scuttered underneath the bushes. But presently, as nothing happened, he came out, and climbed upon a wheelbarrow and peeped over. The first thing he saw was Mr. McGregor hoeing onions. His back was turned towards Peter, and beyond him was the gate!

Peter got down very quietly off the wheelbarrow, and started running as fast as he could go, along a straight walk behind some black-currant bushes.

Mr. McGregor caught sight of him at the corner, but Peter did not care. He slipped underneath the gate, and was safe at last in the wood outside the garden.

Mr. McGregor hung up the little jacket and the shoes for a scare-crow to frighten the blackbirds.

Peter never stopped running or looked behind him till he got home to the big fir-tree.

He was so tired that he flopped down upon the nice soft sand on the floor of the rabbit-hole and shut his eyes. His mother was busy cooking; she wondered what he had done with his clothes. It was the second little jacket and pair of shoes that Peter had lost in a fortnight!

I am sorry to say that Peter was not very well during the evening.

His mother put him to bed, and made some camomile tea; and she gave a dose of it to Peter!

"One table-spoonful to be taken at bed-time."

But Flopsy, Mopsy, and Cotton-tail had bread and milk and blackberries for supper.

THE END

Did you like *The Tale of Peter Rabbit?* There are many more stories about Peter Rabbit. You can find them at the library. They are all by the same writer, Beatrix Potter. She first wrote about Peter Rabbit in 1893. So her stories have lasted a long time.

When Beatrix Potter
First Wrote about Peter Rabbit
by DOROTHY ALDIS

One day when Beatrix Potter picked up her mail, there was a letter from her friend Annie Moore. She knew that Annie's five-year-old son Noel had been very sick. Was he worse?

She read the letter at once.

Dear Beatrix,

Can you imagine a five-year-old being tied down to his bed for months? Noel has been good so far. His father is great at thinking up games for him to play.

But I know we can't go on this way. Besides killing us, it might turn him into a spoiled boy. Noel will have to learn to entertain himself. . . .

171

Beatrix Potter stopped there. She
knew Noel liked stories. And she knew
he liked animals. Maybe she could
write and draw something that would
entertain him. She went straight to
her room and began this letter.

Dear Noel,
    I don't know what to write you.
So I shall tell you a story about four
little Rabbits. Their names were—

Flopsy, Mopsy, Cotton-tail,

and Peter.

They lived with their mother in a sand-bank under the root of a big fir-tree.

Beatrix Potter drew a picture on the first page of her letter. It showed the four little rabbits.

Flopsy, Mopsy, and Peter had ears that stood up. Cotton-tail had ears that were folded back. She looked sleepy that way.

On the second page of the letter was another picture. It showed each rabbit wearing a little coat.

Even with just pen and ink, Beatrix Potter could draw lovely pictures of rabbits.

Noel loved the letter. He thought the story was wonderful.

Beatrix Potter wrote him more letters with more stories about the rabbits. He saved all the letters and all the pictures.

Eight years later Beatrix Potter decided to put her stories into a book. And boys and girls have been reading *The Tale of Peter Rabbit* ever since.

UNIT FOUR

Numbers, Nature, and Nonsense

Tracks in the Snow

by

MARCHETTE CHUTE

This was a mouse who played around
All by himself one night,
Dancing under the winter moon
Forward and left and right.

This was a pheasant walking by,
Out with a friend or two . . .

This was a rabbit running fast,
The way that rabbits do.

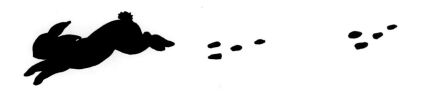

This was a squirrel who found a nut.

This was a chickadee . . .

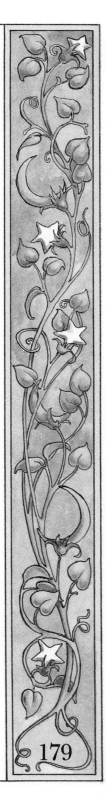

179

And this uncommon sort of track
I think was probably me.

Feet

by

AILEEN FISHER

Feet of snails
are only one.
Birds grow two
to hop and run.
Dogs and cats
and cows grow four.
Ants and beetles
add two more.
Spiders run around
on eight,
which may seem
a lot, but wait—
Centipedes
have more than thirty
feet to wash
when they get dirty.

181

The Purple Cow

by

GELETT BURGESS

I never saw a purple cow.
I never hope to see one.
But I can tell you, anyhow,
I'd rather see than be one.

Rumpelstiltskin

by the

BROTHERS GRIMM

Once upon a time there was a man who had a beautiful daughter.

He wanted the king to meet her.

He knew that the king loved gold. So he said to the king, "My daughter can spin straw into gold."

"That is a fine thing to be able to do," said the king. "Bring your daughter to me. I want to see her spin straw into gold."

The next day the king led the girl
to a room that was full of straw.

"Sit down at this spinning wheel," said
the king. "By morning you must spin all
this straw into gold, or you will die."

The king walked out and shut the door.
The girl began to cry.

All at once the door opened again, and
in came a little man. He said, "You look
sad, my girl. What is wrong?"

"My father told the king that I could
spin straw into gold," she said. "I cannot.
No one can spin straw into gold."

"I can," said the little man. "What will
you give me if I spin it for you?"

"My necklace," said the girl.

He took her necklace. Then he started spinning. He kept spinning all night.

By morning there was no more straw, and the room was full of gold.

The king was very happy.

He took the girl into a bigger room.

It was filled with straw.

Again he said, "Spin all this straw into gold by morning, or you must die."

When he left, the girl looked at the straw. She shook her head sadly.

Then the door opened. The little man came in again. "What will you give me if I spin for you tonight?" he asked.

"I will give you my ring," said the girl.

So the little man took the ring.

By morning he had finished spinning all the straw into gold.

The king smiled at all that gold!

He took her into a still larger room. It was full of straw.

"Spin all this straw into gold," said the king. "Then you shall be my wife."

The little man came in again. "What will you give me tonight?" he asked.

"I have nothing left," said the girl.

"Then you must promise me your first child after you are queen," he said.

The girl did not know what else to do, so she promised.

The little man worked all night. He finished spinning all the straw into gold.

When the king saw it, he made the girl his wife at once. So she became queen.

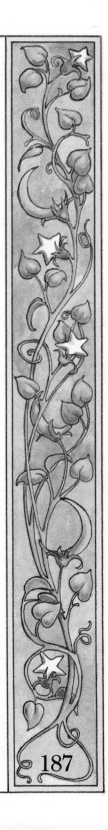

In a year's time she had a beautiful child, and she forgot about the little man.

But one day he came into her room. He said, "Now give me the child that you promised me."

"Oh, no!" cried the queen. "I will give you all my riches, but not my child!"

"No," said the little man. "A living child is worth more than all your riches."

The queen dropped to her knees. She cried, "Please let me keep my child."

"I will give you three days to guess my name," he said. "If you find it out in that time, you may keep your child. But if you do not, the child is mine."

The queen spent all day and all night thinking of names.

When the little man came back, she went through all the names she had ever heard.

But each time she guessed, he said, "No. That is not my name."

The second day, the queen sent out all her helpers to find strange names and bring them to her. She tried many of them on the little man.

"Are you called Horse-legs?" she asked. "Or is your name Sheep-ears? Or Spinning Man?"

But each time he said, "No. That is not my name."

The third day a helper came back.

"I have found only one new name," he told the queen. "As I passed through the woods, I came to a little house. In front of the little house there was a fire. Around the fire danced a strange little man. He hopped on one leg and sang:

'The child is mine.
I've won the game,
For Rumpelstiltskin
Is my name.' "

How happy the queen was to hear that name!

191

She smiled when the little man came back. "Is your name Jack?" she said.

"No," he said. "That is not my name."

"Is your name Harry?" she asked.

"No, no," said the little man.

And then she said, "Are you called RUMPELSTILTSKIN?"

"Who told you that? Who told you?" cried the little man. "No one knows my name."

He stamped his right foot so hard that it sank into the ground. Then he kicked with his left foot so hard that he split in two.

And that was the end of him.

The Secret Sits

by

ROBERT FROST

We dance round in a ring and suppose,
But the Secret sits in the middle and knows.

Twinkle, Twinkle, Little Star

by

JANE TAYLOR

Twinkle, twinkle, little star,
How I wonder what you are.
Up above the world so high,
Like a diamond in the sky.

As your bright and tiny spark
Lights the traveler in the dark,
Though I know not what you are,
Twinkle, twinkle, little star.

195

Star Light, Star Bright

from

AMERICAN MOTHER GOOSE

Star light, star bright,
First star I've seen tonight.
I wish I may, I wish I might
Get the wish I wish tonight.

196

197

Sinbad the Sailor
from the
ARABIAN NIGHTS

Some call me "Sinbad the Sailor." That is a very good name for me, since I have sailed to many lands.

Some call me "Sinbad the Rich Man." That is a good name, too, since my trips have made me wealthy.

Listen, and I shall tell you about my strangest trip. It was long ago.

A storm blew my ship off course. So we landed on the first island we saw and set out to explore it.

I took a side path and picked some fruit to eat. After that, I sat down under a tree and soon fell asleep.

When I woke, I saw my ship, far out at sea. No one had missed me. They had sailed without me. I was alone.

I climbed up a tall tree to see more of the island. In the distance I spotted something that looked like a big white ball. What could it be?

As I drew near it, I saw that it had no door. I tried to climb it, but there were no footholds.

It was round and hard, but warm, and it was two times as tall as I was.

As I walked around this strange ball, the sky grew dark. I looked up.

A giant bird had covered the sun! I had heard of a huge bird called the roc. This ball must be its egg. Sure enough, the bird settled down on the egg.

Its legs were as big as tree trunks.

An idea came to me. Maybe the roc could carry me off this island. Then, maybe I could get back home.

201

When the bird was sleeping, I tried
to tie myself to its leg.

But pull as I would, I feared that
my knots would come loose.

Maybe I would be safer in a sling.
I worked on it all night, with my hopes
rising.

In the morning the giant bird rose
high into the air, carrying me. It flew
to another island. Then it sailed down
into a valley.

When the roc touched the ground,
I untied myself. And not a second too
soon!

The huge bird rose again.

It dropped on a snake and killed it. The roc tore off a piece of snake meat, ate it, and flew away.

The valley was dry, deep, and narrow. The cliffs around it were high and steep. There was no way to climb out.

"If only I had stayed on the other island!" I cried. "There, I had fruit to eat. Here, I have nothing."

I kicked at the stones on the ground. Only then did I notice that each stone twinkled. Each one was a diamond.

Oh, to have such diamonds at home! Home! I would never get home.

Then I saw a smaller roc fly down.

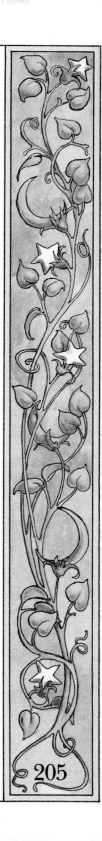

It picked up a piece of the snake.
Then it flew to the top of the cliff.

I knew what I had to do. To leave the
valley, I must be carried again by a bird.

But they landed only to pick up food.
I must tie myself to a piece of the snake.
I shuddered. But it was the only way.

I filled my pockets with diamonds. Then I tied a piece of snake to my back, and I lay face down on the ground.

Soon a roc picked me up. Then it rose to the top of the cliff. It dropped me in its nest and flew off.

At once I untied myself.

From the cliff, I could see a city. I set off and reached it before night. How good it was to see people again!

With one huge diamond, I paid for a ship and sailed home.

Then I gave much money to the poor.

And I still have many diamonds left to remind me of my strangest trip.

Winter Moon
by
LANGSTON HUGHES

How thin and sharp is the
   moon tonight!
How thin and sharp and
   ghostly white
Is the slim curved crook of the
   moon tonight!

The Wind and the Moon

by

GEORGE MacDONALD

Said the Wind to the Moon,

"I will blow you out.

You stare

In the air

Like a ghost in a chair,

Always looking at what I'm about.

I hate to be watched. I'll blow you out."

209

11

De Colores

una canción español tradicional

De colores,
    De colores se visten los campos
    En la primavera.
De colores,
    De colores son los pajaritos
    Que vienen de afuera.
De colores,
    De colores es el arco iris
    Que vemos lucir.

Y por eso los grandes amores
De muchos colores me gustan a mi.

Canta el gallo,
    Canta el gallo con el quiri, quiri
    Quiri, quiri, quiri.
La gallina,
    La gallina con el cara, cara
    Cara, cara, cara.
Los polluelos,
    Los polluelos con el pio, pio
    Pio, pio, pio.

Many Colors

a traditional Spanish folk song

Colorful,
How colorfully the fields are dressed
In the spring.
Colorful,
How colorful are the little birds
That come from the countryside.
Colorful,
How colorful is the rainbow
That we see shining.

And I love all these things because
Their many colors are pleasing to me.

The rooster sings,
The rooster sings with a quiri, quiri
Quiri, quiri, quiri.
The hen,
The hen with a cara, cara
Cara, cara, cara.
The baby chicks,
The baby chicks with a pio, pio
Pio, pio, pio.

211

Stone Soup for Sharing

from a

SCANDINAVIAN FOLKTALE

There was once a man who traveled far and wide. He made friends wherever he went. "It is because of my magic stone," he would say. But his friends knew that it was more than just his magic stone.

One day, when he was hungry, he came to a little house in the woods.

"How good it would feel to sit down and eat with the family who lives here," he said. He knocked at the door.

The mother came to see who it was. Her son and daughter were behind her.

"Good evening," said the man. "I have walked far. I would thank you if you would let me sit down and have a meal with you."

The woman shook her head. "I have just enough food for my family. There is nothing left to share with a stranger."

213

"Let me share my magic stone with you," said the man. "With it, I can make stone soup."

The woman was surprised. "Soup from a stone? That would be wonderful. But I don't see how it could be done."

"Bring me a big pot," said the man. "And I will show you how to make stone soup."

Before the woman could answer, her daughter hurried to get a pot.

"It will be good to learn how to make soup from a stone," said the girl. "Please, Mother. Let's find out how to do it."

"Is it good?" her little brother asked.

"Stone soup is a meal fit for a king," he said. "Fill the pot with water, please."

The girl did as he asked. Then she placed the pot on the fire.

He dropped his stone into the pot. Then he began to stir the water.

"Let me help you," the woman said. "I do love good thick soup."

"Well," said the man. "I've used this stone many times. So this soup may not be very thick. If only I had a bit of flour to put in, I could make it thicker."

"I'll get you a bit of flour," said the woman. She hurried to fetch it for him.

Little by little, he added it to the water. Then he took a taste.

"Ah," said the man. "That is better. It is getting thicker. But this soup would be better yet with just a bit of rice and meat in it."

"We have some rice," the girl said.

"What about the leftover meat from last night?" said her brother.

She brought back the rice and meat.
The man thanked her. Then he
added the rice and meat to his soup.

And he kept on stirring.

He tasted it and smiled. "Ah," he said.
"If only I had a carrot. Or some peas.
With carrots and peas, this might be the
best pot of stone soup I have ever made."

"I can pull up some carrots from my garden," said the boy.

The girl got a small bag of peas.

The man added them to the soup.

The woman never took her eyes off the pot. "What fine soup we shall have. And all from a stone!" she added with a smile.

After some time, the man tasted the soup again. "It is ready," he said. "This stone soup is fit for a king."

He gave it one more stir. "Of course," he added, "the king has bread and butter with his soup."

"And so will we," said the woman. She brought out brown bread and butter.

Never had the family liked a meal so much! The boy and girl kept laughing and saying, "All from a stone."

"Thank you, friend," said the woman. "That was a happy meal we shared. I would like to make stone soup again."

"I will leave my magic stone with you," he said. "But now I must be on my way."

Then off he went. Soon he picked up a stone from the road and put it in his pocket. And he smiled, thinking how the magic of sharing turns strangers into friends.

A·C·K·N·O·W·L·E·D·G·M·E·N·T·S

Acknowledgment is gratefully made to the following individuals and publishers for permission to reprint these selections.

"Nonsense A B C Rhymes." Reprinted by permission from *Beginner's Bookshelf: The Illustrated Treasury of Children's Literature,* Volume I, edited by Margaret E. Martignoni, © 1965 and 1982 by J. G. Ferguson Publishing Company, 111 East Wacker Drive, Chicago, Illinois 60601.

"The Pledge to the Flag." From *Uncle Sam and the Flag.* Reprinted by permission of Oddo Publishing.

"Animal Crackers." Excerpt in "Animal Crackers" from *Songs for a Little House* by Christopher Morley. © 1917, 1945 by Christopher Morley. Reprinted by permission of Harper & Row, Publishers, Inc.

The Tale of Peter Rabbit. Text from *The Tale of Peter Rabbit* by Beatrix Potter (Frederick Warne & Company, 1902), © Frederick Warne & Company, 1902. Reprinted by permission of Penguin Books Ltd.

"When Beatrix Potter Wrote about Peter Rabbit." Excerpted from *Nothing Is Impossible: The Story of Beatrix Potter.* © 1969 Mary Cornelia Aldis Porter. Reprinted by permission of Atheneum Publishers, an imprint of Macmillan Publishing Company.

"Tracks in the Snow." From *Around and About* by Marchette Chute. © 1957 by E. P. Dutton, Inc. Copyright renewed 1985 by Marchette Chute. Reprinted by permission of the author.

"Feet." From *Cricket in a Thicket* by Aileen Fisher. © 1963 by Aileen Fisher. Reprinted by permission of the author.

"The Secret Sits." © 1942 by Robert Frost. © 1970 by Lesley Frost Ballantine. Reprinted from *The Poetry of Robert Frost,* edited by Edward Connery Lathem, by permission of Henry Holt and Company, Inc.

"Star Light, Star Bright." From *American Mother Goose,* published by J. B. Lippincott.

I·L·L·U·S·T·R·A·T·I·O·N C·R·E·D·I·T·S

Acknowledgment is gratefully made to the following for permission to reprint these illustrations.

PAGE	ILLUSTRATOR
11–19, 20	Jerry Pinkney. © 1991 by Jamestown Publishers, Inc. All rights reserved.
21	Kate Greenaway. Reprinted by permission of The Huntington Library, San Marino, California.
23	N. C. Wyeth. Courtesy of the Delaware Museum, Helen Farr Sloan Library.
25	Arthur Rackham.
26–27, 29	Pamela R. Levy. © 1991 by Jamestown Publishers, Inc. All rights reserved.
31	Arthur Rackham. Rare Book Department, Free Library of Philadelphia.
33–34	Tasha Tudor. Illustrations of Thumbelina reprinted by permission of Grosset & Dunlap from *Tasha Tudor's Book of Fairy Tales,* © 1961 by Platt & Munk Company, Inc., © renewed 1989 by Tasha Tudor.
35	Jessie Willcox Smith.
37	Alfred Augustus Glendening. © Courtesy of Art Licensing International.
39	Milo Winter. From *The Aesop for Children,* illustrated by Milo Winter. © 1919, 1947 Checkerboard Press, a division of Macmillan, Inc. All rights reserved.
41–42, 48, 50	W. Heath Robinson.
43, 45	Arthur Rackham.
53	Arthur Rackham. Arthur Rackham Collection, Rare Book and Manuscript Library, Columbia University.

222

224